beehiv

E. Alicia

E. Alicia

ISBN-13: 978-1541250185
ISBN-10: 1541250184

beehive

for you, my bee.

E. Alicia

beehive

[Note]

Bodies can be dormant for years. I learned this recently. I transitioned from child to adult. Once. I was me and then me, but bigger. I thought *this is it.* But there are red buttons within each of us which read **s e l f d e s t r u c t** and sometimes the gentlest knock can cause them to be pushed. As people, we are seekers. We seek answers to who we are, we question ourselves, our lives, *is this it?* At the age of twenty-two I have lived the life of three people. The other two are sisters who have left home. One day they might return, perhaps without warning or welcome, but I won't anticipate them, they are free spirits. I have stopped asking *who am I?* because I have tried to find myself more than once and, just as I began to get used to my own company, I was gone. I am no philosopher. I have not graduated with a degree from **'the university of life'** (as my dad says). But who does? We all die before we graduate from there; no professors are left to lecture us. Just remember that people change. We do not question the transition of child to adult, so why do we question the transition from adulthood to adulthood to adulthood? Let people be. Change with them. Let's look at one another through stained glass windows and see each other's multitude of colours and instead of ask *who am I?* ask *am I happy in this moment?* and let the answer always be **'yes'**.

E. Alicia

beehive

[Another Note]

'What is destined will reach you, even if it be beneath two mountains. What is not destined will not reach you, even if it be between your two lips.'

Al-Ghazali

We are alive in a beehive. We are bees. We live together, work together, breathe together. We sting and we get stung, by lovers and life. We taste sweetness and we become sweet. Enjoy the yellowness of the year and endure its blackness, but do not waste your time seeking either, because *they* will find *you*.

Somewhere, there is a dark room filled with string and on every line hangs a long series of photographs yet to develop. We are undeveloped. Only the photographer knows who we are.

Stop looking.

E. Alicia

beehive

Sometimes
I wake up and poetry has

Se e p   e   d
through my pores and stained the sheets.

To write it down
is to clean it up.

       -    *what a mess.*

E. Alicia

i have learned to love the extra parts of me.
i have learned how to break.
how to heal.
how to pray.

i am grateful to the women
who said what i was too scared to say.
to make ok what i was too scared to think.
to remind me that it is beautiful
to watch the snow outside
whilst I glow
within.

-   *poetry*

E. Alicia

to our Queen.
You have been stung so many times
by her
and him
and me.

send us away.

we will leave and return with
flowers, nectar sweet.
remember
every day,
this hive

worships at
Your feet.

- Mother

E. Alicia

beehive

the sweetness

Honey

noun

A sweet, sticky brown fluid made by bees.

- Your honey made me sweet.

I was one of those toys you find in the kids stores
with *try me* scratched in bold across my palms.

I was paid for.

But you knew which buttons to press.

-    *I wanted you*

I will never forget the feeling
of being held by you
for the first time.

You were behind me,
with your arms around my waist,
your perfect fingers interlaced
across my stomach as if you
were praying in
the only way I knew
back then.

I pretended to admire the view,
the fields were empty
and in that moment
I never felt so free.

You turned me around
and kissed me.

I could still taste the salt on your lips.

-   *where were we?*

I cried.
Not with sadness
or relief.
My eyes spilled on their own.
All of the holes on my face poured.
Tears and snot and
sweat and sick
slid.

I had read that it's hard to stay silent.
I was proud of my throat
fingers
mind and
I was applauded by the
flushing
of a chain. I felt beautiful.
For a second

until six months on and with
raw fingers
I cleared the fog
from the bathroom mirror,
only to reveal
a frosted tongue
and that the steam from the shower
had curled the ends of my hair.

- *saved*

you have called me sweetheart
when every inch of me was sour.
you have never winced at the acidic taste of a tongue tucked
behind ripe lips.
you have stayed
despite knowing that
each time you taste the bitterness
will not be the last because
your tongue will bleed each time you bite it.
you have stayed
and stirred me with your honey.
i won't forget.

-     *thank you*

you grew a mango tree and
picked the fruit
too soon,
green with sickness,
it was hardened to the
core.

you left it by the window,
in the sunlight for
nine months and
rolled it in your palms
in the evenings

until eventually,
you opened it up
and smelled its sugar.
you squeezed its ripened
flesh between your fingertips
and

cupped its skin, as though you
held the globe,
to suck the pulp.
its juices
flowed
like syrup
down
your chin.

- *I am the mango*

you taught me the value of skin,

that it is ok for my soft fingertips to skim the
swelling ripples in the tide.

nine months after I met you,
my hips curved into a

w i d e   s m i l e

to say thank you.

-     *acceptance*

you have always glided through my body,
barefoot and
naked,
listening to the padded echo of soft skin
on marble floor.

I am vast,
I am hollow,
I am white washed.

you furnish me,
you sit down to eat,
you lick your fingertips,

you sleep.

-   *home*

I dream about waking every morning, sticky with heat.
I want to wake up coated in sugar and sheets. To have to
peel my fingertips from honeyed skin. To feel warm breath
from parted lips on pale cheeks. To bury my nose
in his neck and smell slumber deep and musky, inhale yesterday's
scent dragged into the heaps of cotton; I'd bathe in it. Its residue
on my skin, like the traces left from a thousand tiny
kisses on porcelain. I don't want to leave. I could spend
a full day, counting his eyelashes, the creases in his lips,
letting my hands run over chest and ribs and hips and further
down, to his feet. I would shower in him, and when I was done,
I would not leave. I would sleep, heavy in his arms and
his arms heavy on me. I will not leave.
A world outside of this raft does not await,
there is no land to see.
My world is here,
dreaming
beside me.

-     *What do you dream?*

i was weathered,
scratched.
i could tear a man,
slice his skin
or puncture him
with my enamel but
you came and
cracked the strength from me
and now my beauty stands out
against your mahogany.

-     *I am ivory*

I'll put you between my lips and
inhale you.
Like you do with that cigarette
every night before you go to
sleep.

- *my addiction*

People are jigsaws.
Parts that fit.

Look down at your left hand and stretch your palms.

      Look at the

crevice

      between your thumb and your index finger.

You were made for me.

- *we fit*

They thought you'd fractured your wrist once
and all I could think was

my bones have been split since the day I

    fell

    a thousand feet in love with you.

- it hurt

beehive

we

drip

from one another's lips

I am milk

and you are honey

-   *you're sweet*

There are going to be
days
and nights
and weeks
when my words scratch
your honeyed skin
and sugar seeps from your eyes
and down
your honeyed cheeks.

You can take days
and nights
and weeks.
I will kneel at your feet,
my lips will kiss,
my tongue will lick,
my throat will choke
'I'm sorry'
until you come
back to me.

- *worship*

I have watched your hands feed and clothe,
pat backs, catch fists, write notes.
They have tidied, wiped windows, cleaned floors and
I have watched them roll
and light cigarettes to sit between someone else's lips,
carry bags filled with someone else's things,
direct, soothe, protect.
I have watched you hold men taller in height,
wider in stature,
but not stronger in strength or heart, than you.

I have watched your hands hold the wheel, drive us home,
I have felt the warmth of them in mine,
they have opened doors for me, pulled out thrones for me,
they have wiped my tears, slid
down my back, tangled in my hair,
wrapped around my neck,
I have felt them inside of me.
Your hands have steadied me,
tilted my head,
held up my world
and your hands have made me promises:

they will hold sons with fists the same as yours,
a daughter with your life etched in her palms.

Yet you feel inferior,
when my hands could never
touch hearts
like yours.

    -   *hands*

Your mother didn't name you for nothing.
You are a warrior.

With Your knowledge and strength,
You can conquer anything. Even this.

-    *grief*

He has always held so much authority
in the way he walks.
There is power in his steps,
in his feet.
It touches the insides of me,
like a thousand tiny fingers,
the wings of a bee,
a tide
in my stomach,
I am weak at the knees.

He isn't. He strides.
Glides through rooms and
turns the lights on. I see people's
eyes widening as he flicks the switches,
gives them vision, but nobody watches
him like me, in awe of the way he moves,
the way he sweeps through life,
melts through doors like butter.
He is my answered prayer.
He is prey.
I could watch him all day.

I'll feast on him later.

-    *watching you work*

The best day of my life was
any day I have touched you.

\-   *obsessed.*

How do you know you're in love?

Because I am
terrified.

- *are you scared too?*

You kiss my lips,
my neck, my chest, my hips,
stomach, feet, fingertips
you suck
you lick
caress
spit

I'm scared you'll bite.

-   *don't hurt me.*

The only shame I'll bring you
is that I will love you more
than you could ever.

      -   *Always*

I know it washed you down
to know the pearl you wanted
was in the belly of another shell.

I know it slices you open
to see salt caught in the flecks
of silver on her cheeks.

I know it disembowels you
to taste the acid spilling from
her serpent tongue.

I know it drains your blood
to smell the doubt which
seeps from her pores.

I know it scrapes you out
to feel disapproving eyes on
your brown hands against paper.

I know it stuffs you full
to hear your father choke
on her name.

I know it seals you up again
to lose your senses, knowing
that she'll be by your side

forever.

-    *your gut is the sixth sense*

You say

I love the way you say my name.

That's because the letters spill from a white mouth and I pronounce the

sy lla bles

different to your mother.

There's a reason why your name sounds like
honey from my lips:

Each time our tongues touch,
I drink your syrup and
when I praise or curse or beckon you
the warrior drips from my tongue,
your knowledge runs down my chin
and it sounds like pleasure because
one day,
I will be exalted too.

      -    *our name*

i keep writing.
so the day my white
melts beneath her eyes and
she utters **she's not good enough,**
i can hand her this book and
she will read it.

she will realise our love survived
a year at sea
without a raft.

if you are reading this,
know that **i am good.**
nobody could love your son **enough.**

     -   *to his mother*

if they read my words
before they saw my mouth,
they'd love me.

-     *his parents.*

I'd go

Back

Just to relive the dawn and
days and nights that were forbidden.

Just to appreciate your face for the first time.

Just to feel invincible. To share our secret
just with us.

Not because I enjoyed the pain.

I'd just like to get to know you again

And again and again and again

-   *I never stopped to admire the view*

beehive

You've travelled this globe
on foot
and I have moved around you.

Do you like what you have seen?

-    *earth and sun*

under three degrees

and I was still burning inside.

weren't you?

- *at night*

One night

I want you to pick me up
and drive me to the trees.

I want you to pretend I'm the girl you used to know.
The girl you never got to know.
Watch me burn on your back seats.
Sit beside her and let her flames lick you,
let her patent you.
She'll show you what it feels like to ignite.
She'll show you what could have been
had she not destroyed herself in her own fire.

Her ashes are soft. You kept those.

- *new me*

E. Alicia

I feel that I need nothing in this life,
of this life,
than words.
Flowers on a page.
Roses and
white lilies.
Words make beautiful
both the thorns and velvet of love
and the pale face of death.

Through words, the world is
illuminated.
A bouquet
to say what the mouth could
wilt.

I need nothing more.

- *beauty*

My grandmother used to draw me flowers.
Grown up, I received them from my love.

They were prettier on the page.

Like words.

- *words*

beehive

the sting

A bee only stings when it feels threatened.

- *i didn't mean to torment you.*

I was naïve to think so much sugar
wouldn't make me sick.

- ~~naïve~~ *hopeful*

that's an unusual name,
they say.
i explain,
and they want to close
their ears like they
close their mouths.
their eyes mime

be careful,

brown skin is sticky.

-   *judgement*

you have always glided through my body,
barefoot and
naked.

You made me your home and
for so long, I thought that it was beautiful
that you felt comfortable enough to reside in my
chest,
to sleep there.
But I have spent three nights awake
with the weight of you.
I now realise,

you never even knocked and
I never welcomed you in.

-   *Intruder*

If a man ever steps into your body without welcome,

threaten to step into his mother's home
whilst you're still his secret.

you'll see him turn white, like you.

- *to sisters stuck in honey.*

beehive

A bee stings in defence.
To protect its hive from an intruder.
To defend its colony.

-    *are you protecting your family from me?*

- or protecting me from your family?

fear is
being scared to tell your mother that you are in love with a white
girl.

cowardice is
not telling her.

- *She'll never know*

I had an affair
and you're still having one.

-    *being a secret hurts*

So, you say I am your everything.

How can a person be *everything*
when they aren't part of every thing
you do.

everything should mean I sleep inside
the crevices
upon your skin
and inside your soul.
everything should mean I'm sewn
into your days
and your sheets.

I'm not your everything.
I'm not part of *anything*
except for 'us'.
I'm an entirely different life.

-    *anything and everything*

beehive

White girls are sugar.

>Did your mother
>ever tell you
>too much sugar rots your teeth?

>>Your cheeks are honeyed

>>>and I have
>>>toothache.

\-   *too much of a good thing.*

you used to sneak me out
and to hear your car exhaust past midnight
got the pit of my stomach
rattling with it.
wet kisses,
wet lips,
wet fingers.
in the excitement,
i was always trying to catch my breath.
i was high on the fumes of
aftershave and sex.

yesterday was my twenty-second birthday and
you snuck me out
of the back door of
a restaurant
and down a fire escape
beside the bins because
a man who knows your family was feeding
downstairs.
the cold air
caught my breath.
the comedown kills me.

- *sneak*

tiredness
headaches
friends and family

i shut the lid,
you swallow the key.

-    *reasons you leave*

being lonely

and

being   alone

are different.

In the end,
        I left
because being with you
was the loneliest togetherness
I ever felt.

        -   *distance*

When I met you, I couldn't cry.
Now I cry too much.

No doubt it was you who snapped the pipe
and with it, the words came flooding.

    -   *tears*

don't leave ite(me)s
unattended.

    -   *there are thieves around*

it's the twenty-second year and one day of my life
and I am sitting on the edge
of a bed made for
two people.
the room is a mess
with the clothes i
scattered
last night whilst
dressing a body
for you.

- *bad memories*

E. Alicia

I have started to miss your fingers

so I have used my own instead.

- *wretch*

It's the hardest at night
when the backs of my eyes
dance.

what scares me is that
i find my way to the woods
in the darkness.

you know what i mean.

-    *jinns*

E. Alicia

You gave up on me once when you left me desperate with
i need you.

Twice when
i checked your car was home
but not that I was safe.

Three times when
i can't do this anymore, it's over

because living with the devil in my head

was too difficult for **you.**

-    *I*

you left me

at the edge of the water

surrounded by trees

in the dark.

I needed you

                    and we were this far apart.

-    *too far apart*

Maybe I'm mad
because grandma used to let us
play in the woods as
children.

I want to go to the woods tonight.

Maybe, all those years ago,
something crawled inside of me
and beckons me
back.

I want to go to the woods tonight.

That's when I feel closest to myself.

Right now, I have lost my own mind.

- *I scare myself.*

When you leave
I am left clawing at the windows.
I am left staring at the creases of your lips,
imprinted on the edge of a half empty glass.
I am left sat in the warmth your body left.
Your sweetness clings to me, and I swear
I can still feel the dampness of your breath
between my thighs.
My body draws away from itself,
pulls my skin towards the door and begs me
to re-trace the steps we've taken,
to drive through dark streets,
feel the exhale of country air,
let it wash away the smell of stale cigarettes
you left in my hair.
And when I arrive at *anywhere*
I can sink to my knees beneath the canopy
as though in prayer.
But I am wailing.
Picking at skin and soil.
I have stones in my teeth
and salt in my eyes
and I can see the water
lit by my headlights.
The earth has made me brown.
I want the fingers of leaves to feel like yours.
Because when you leave
I get lodged in the throat of loneliness,
loneliness that no other body could correct
but yours but you're absent
and the next best thing to you,
whilst you sleep in the arms of your other life,
is for me to be held
by any ground we've walked on.

-   *driven crazy*

E. Alicia

~~Most days~~

on the days you want to see me
I look at you and think

What have I done?

-   *regrets*

When you're here, my brain is laced with so many beautiful
words, a string of them, like a daisy chain and I think

you must remember to write these down.

But then you go.
and I forget them.

and the daisies die and rot so slowly, I don't notice.

I'm left without a good word to say. and that is why
this book is filled with rotten daisies.
it's a cycle.
it's a chain.
because you leave.

　　　-　*daisy chain*

You know, I can't remember what alone felt like.

but lonely is all too familiar.

     -   *alonely*

I showered spices from my hair and
scrubbed York from my skin
with salt.

It is over now.
And I miss your fingers.

- *time flies*

i never know if i'll wake in the morning and you'll want me

back.

- *decide.*

as much as
i love
the khaki
of your jacket,
its reflection is uncanny
in your eyes.

-   *Jealousy*

You have touched
but not adored for so long that you
do not know how to love, even when
you feel it.
Those frayed fingers, which have
left their greasy prints on so many legs
and arms
and around so many necks

        and slid across so many chests

cannot touch a heart,
or

      slip into the palms of a woman
who loves you to the knuckles,
to the ends of an earth filled with masculinity,
not a

      single
one a man
but

      you,
if you do not unveil it,
will lose your grip on me,

      slip your fingers out of me
and you will never find this feeling
of hope, of lust, of fire at the
pit again.
You will regret.
You will mourn.
You will touch
but not adore for so long that you
will never know how to love,
and you will never feel it
again.

- be careful

right now

i never want to marry you.

-    *nor anybody else*

it's over.

the acid in my throat burns with my fingers
by the bonfire.

\-   *I promise I'll never take you back*

beehive

I break that promise every time.

What would you change about me?

I wish you'd pray more.

-   *for this to work.*

Ivory is expensive.
Diamond's gleam.

I am not milk,

I am cream.

-   *I deserve ~~the universe~~*

it will be like cutt
ing ribbon
from a height.
your half will
fall
and land
lim
     p.
mine will be
f r a y e d
at the
       end.

    -   *when i'm ready*

beehive

When you said

I like your nails

I should have scratched you.

      -   *a scratch for a sting.*

your lips are freshly licked postage stamps,
they'll never lose their stick
with me.

they're curling at the corners when you ask
if I still think you're a
bad boy.

you know the answer. pride is spilling
out in your spit and I wonder *why* I subjected myself
to this.

-    *concrete to the core.*

beehive

My mother says
that you have given her an open mindedness.

- *at least some good came out of this mess.*

i saw you.

in a supermarket.
you were there with your quiet wife.
she was pregnant
and you had a knee-high girl at your feet.

you wanted a boy.

do you do with her
what you did with me?

when you recognised these eyes
loose hair
and hips
I was greeted with wet lips
and lust.
even now,
it's still deceit.
you couldn't keep me then

but you've always wanted me.

- *prediction*

my patent is different.
i carry different scars.
i smoulder
instead of burn.

i am snow
instead of earth.

and they don't know me.

and they don't *want* to know me.

- *colour*

one day, you'll arrive home and
find me with your mother
at your table.

she will introduce me.

and you will have to act as though
you have never laid brown eyes
on this pretty white face before.

careful you don't drool when
your mother makes you say

Hello.

    -   *watch me*

It brings me so much pain
to see that I still have so much space
between my knuckles
on the ring finger of my left hand.

I'm in agony.

And I remind myself daily
you didn't do this for him,
you stupid, stupid girl

but he was mine and
he is perfect.

I feel like showing up
at his mother's front door
with
just marry me
written in mehndi
across my head.

because I miss his fingers
like the ring finger on my
left hand misses a ring.

- *pain*

Do you know what I have learned
in writing words?

      That I have unhappiness knitted into me.

Do you know what I have learned
in writing words?

      That you are knitted into them. To me.

Do you know what I have learned
in writing words?

      That I should leave and let myself be happy.

Do you know what I have learned
in writing words?

      The wool is too strong.
      I can't cast you off.

-   *Do you enjoy torturing me?*

How is it possible to be heart br o ken
when you are somebody's?

-     *anything is possible.*

I deserve the world.

Grass, trees, soil.

All you have given me is the ocean.
and I even cried *that* myself.

-    *self-pity*

broken girls find
mended boys
with stitched minds and
soldered hearts.

these boys try to fix us

like they fixed themselves,
lacing cuts with liquor and
rubbing salt in sores.

they patch us up

using glue to fuse the
splintered parts of us,
tape to put pressure
on our wounds.

but the glue
only sticks them
in our minds
and they only tape
our mouths.

- *sisters*

t r u s t

is only one letter from

t r u t h

- *lies*

I brought so many bags
when I came to live
in your life and they
were heavy
with habit and heart.

They split

and spilt

and stained.

- *you didn't clean them up.*

you dragged a tragic history into a new year.

your history with female anatomy

displaced as mine and i

fell for it

harder than i fell for you.

but now i know that

new years needn't mean

new me.

the me I was before was so beautiful.

hearing you say

it's over,

sounded better than

any sweet word you ever

whispered in my ear,

better than the sound of

the ice cream van,

better than the sound of

any song played

on a midnight drive

with you.

i am on a new road now,

in a faster car

with better music.

it's over

sounds so tuneful

in my mind

and tastes sweeter than

any honey

that has ever passed

my lips.

- *it's over*

every day

I took you at

face value

but you didn't value

my face

when you lied to it.

- *the honest truth*

beehive

I used to see you and pray
let him

marry me

      marry me

         marry me

now I pray
thank God
thank God
thank God

a diamond ring would have been so heavy
and
my heart is heavy enough.

- *weight*

I split my throat last night.

My words were fists.
Stronger.

My screams were gunfire.
Louder.

I was shouting to God.

Begging you to
let me go
and
love me
all at once.

You called me mad.
A woman possessed.
But can't you see?
It was
you
who possessed me.

So pour spite
on your *own* creation
and ignite it.

Set me free.

- *lunacy*

I am

crazy

for you

and

because

of you.

- *insanity*

I have tried to tread ground
we haven't walked on together.
I'm accidentally on purpose
taking every step as déjà vu.
Sometimes I think the only place
we didn't walk
was over the moon.

- remember

I only eat halal meat now

and he is haram.

- always has been

some days i believe
i will never finish this poetry.
words are stirred, thick inside of me.
there will never be enough
to fill my journey.

- *living poetry*

beehive

there has been more sting
than sweetness,
more acid
than alkaline,
more sour milk
than honey.

- *how much 'too much' is enough?*

E. Alicia

the sacrifice

and he found you lost
and guided you.

93:7

The honey bee sacrifices itself and
leaves the hive it's always known, abandons
the sweet sugar it's always made,
to save another bee.

I sacrificed myself and
left my community, I
stopped licking sugar off my fingertips,
to love you.

- *sacrifice*

You once asked me if I had ever tried a samosa
and I laughed.
You seem to think that we're a whole universe apart and
a pastry showed me that.
I have been kneaded into your culture since birth and
twenty-one years have passed, and
only now do I realise
why I never fitted in,
why my white skin was detached.

- *It's just skin*

My modesty
lends itself to words,
to actions un-acted and hands which
slip to the base of one spine,
through the hair on one head,
fingers licked by the mouth of
one love,
which press the lips on one face,
but my own lips will not be pressed.

Those same hands prepare and pray.
Those same hands will hold blessings,
created by the only time my legs
are ever parted.
Closed knees.
Open eyes and ears
which strip me of naivety and let me
bathe in modesty
before it clothes me.

My hair can fall without my grace.
My cells will mark my freedom,
my ankles are not chained.
I trust myself and you should
trust me too,
because whilst my modesty is not loud,
nor is it soft,
it lends itself to words uttered through

parted lips, to spread
'no'
to all but my world,
who knows that I am his.

-    *modesty*

I woke before the dawn
to a sticky heat between my thighs,
sickly sweet like cranberries,
it had spread like fire.
Stained sheets.
A snake, skin shed

I used my hands to bathe.

-   *purified*

Nowadays
i say keema instead of minced meat
and my throat fights to say
bismillah
before i eat.

-    *what have you done to me?*

there is a Dua
for scorpion sting.

mix water with
salt
like tears

    Al-Kafirun

    Al-Falaq

    An-Nas

we should say it.

    -   *stung*

it scares me to think that my father's blood runs
through my veins. Intoxicants are haram.

> - '*Do not let your hands*
> *be the cause of your own destruction*'
>
> *2:195*

My	days	stretch	out	ahead	of	me	and
panic	rises	in	my	throat	to	think	about
how	I	could	possibly	fill	the	hours.	

I need routine.

And what gives me more routine than to pray?

- *It makes sense.*

There was a reason for us,
thank God.
It wasn't wasted.

    -   *Reasons*

E. Alicia

I fear God

because he brought me so much pain
in meeting you.

- *omnipotent*

beehive

I have cried myself to raw eyes, red lips and plugged nose
since I found God.
Sometimes I think he's punishing me
for taking so long.

- *sorry*

You may find me again, one day.

- *God Willing*

Dear you.

You used to say that you didn't believe in orthodox religion
like you'd tried them all.
You used to say that you didn't believe in collective worship
like you used to pray.
You used to say that you'd made your own religion
like you were Blake.

You'd only tasted one, and it was bitter
and it had put you off trying the rest.

You read Al-Baqarah and your eyes melted over it
like someone had stolen the words from you.

All along,
this was your religion.
I can't believe you only just figured it out.
Dear me.

- *monotheism*

I was born tonight
and I had a sister
waiting to hold me.

- R

I have accepted,
that before now,
I was searching
high and low
for something
which was beside me
the whole time.

-     *'And he is with you
wherever you are.'*

57:4

I took one step.
He took ten.
I started to walk
and he ran.

-    *Hadith*

I am an exhibition.
Proof.
That a flower
grown in sand
in the Middle East,
a land associated with
tanned skin and sun
and heat,
can be uprooted and planted
in snow

and still flourish
there.

- the two 'r's

Why do I expect levitation,
to grow thickened skin on my feet,
to find my fingers callus and
my knees brown?

I should know
that I am in the same body I was given.
Just grounded
and softened
and cleansed.

- *the same*

My world is thick
now.
The edges rounded.
I'm coated in cotton,
heaps of it,
and it warms me,
melts my heart.

Every night
I say thank you
aloud
and

He whispers back
you're welcome.

- *for the first time,*
  I feel at peace.

I can say goodbye to the words now.

Make sure that you read them for what they are.
A journey
which brought me
to you
to me
to God.

- *God has willed it*

Indeed what is to come will be better than
what has gone by.

93:4

E. Alicia

every drop of honey
was written on days when
life was as
clear and sweet
as its texture.

every sting
was written through wet eyes and
gritted teeth.

you would not have cried,
but I am stung
with emotion.

He rubbed salt on my wounds
and I writhed in pain

but it healed me.

I have been poisoned,
I have become the poison
and he still drinks me every day
and coats me in kisses,
honey sweet.

- I love you

I am sorry
that I was too much
and at the same time
not enough.

- *heavy heart*

T o s e t t h e m f r e e h a s
k e p t m y v e i n s f r o m **clotting.**
my stomach from split   ting
and my mind from ti   p
t   o
            e i n g
away.

   -   *words*

She is my woman and I, her man.

Intertwined bodies of particles that existed before time began.

Through time and space, single atoms, travelled together to create us as one.

Souls combined, completing us whole, together, forever.

- *you wrote that.*

beehive

Printed in Great Britain
by Amazon